A ROOKIE READER

SHINE, SUN!

By Carol Grèene

Illustrations by Gene Sharp

Prepared under the direction of Robert Hillerich, Ph.D.

CHILDRENS PRESS ™

CHICAGO

This book is for Jordan.

Library of Congress Cataloging in Publication Data

Greene, Carol.
  Shine, sun!

  (Rookie reader)
  Includes index.
  Summary: As a child talks to the sun, the reader
can see some of the sun's happy effects.
  [1. Sun—Fiction]   I. Title.   II. Series.
PZ7.G82845Sh   1983   [E]   82-19853
ISBN 0-516-02038-2

Sun? Sun?
Are you there?

There you are!

Here I come.

Hi, sun!

Shine, sun!

Make flowers grow.

Make birds sing.

Make butterflies dance.

Shine on me, sun.

Make me dance too.

Dance in sun.

Dance in shade.

Oh, sun!
Dance with shadow!

Sun? Sun?

Are you there?

There you are.

Hī, sun.

Shine, sun!

Make water warm.

Shine, sun!
Shine on me.

27

Oh, sun!
OUCH!

WORD LIST

are	I	shine
birds	in	sing
butterflies	make	sun
come	me	there
dance	on	too
flowers	oh	warm
grow	ouch	water
here	shade	with
hi	shadow	you

About the Author

Carol Greene has written over 20 books for children, plus stories, poems, songs, and filmstrips. She has also worked as a children's editor and a teacher of writing for children. She received a B.A. in English Literature from Park College, Parkville, Missouri, and an M.A. in Musicology from Indiana University. Ms. Greene lives in St. Louis, Missouri. When she isn't writing, she likes to read, travel, sing, do volunteer work at her church — and write some more. Her *The Super Snoops and the Missing Sleepers*, and *Sandra Day O'Connor, First Woman on the Supreme Court*, have also been published by Childrens Press.

About the Artist

Gene Sharp grew up in Iowa and now lives and works near Chicago. He has illustrated several books in the Rookie Reader series for Childrens Press including *Too Many Balloons, Please, Wind?* and *Hi, Clouds*.